Son of a Beach

©2017 Michael Bournazian
Published by Flowerpublishing
ISBN 978-1-927914-84-7

All rights reserved. No part of this book may be reproduced, stored in a retrieval system or transmitted in any form or by any means without the prior permission of the publisher or author, except by reviewer who may quote brief passages for a review to be printed in a magazine, journal and newspaper.

FLOWERPUBLISHING

MONTREAL, CANADA

WWW.FLOWERPUBLISH.COM

Acknowledgements

Perouz Kouyoumdjian (Mom)
Haroutioun Bournazian (Dad)
Louise Chalmers
Endre Farkas
Michelle Sullivan
MaryAnn Hayatian
FlowerPublishing
Etc.

Dedication

To Mom and Dad (Ma and Ba)

CONTENTS

Grave
-14-

Considerate Crime
-15-

Thin Line Between Eating The Crumbs Under The Toaster And Eating What The Cat Dragged In
-16-

Love In The Eighties
-19-

The 24-Year Chasm
-20-

Your Brittle End
-22-

No Reasons Why
-24-

You Don't Have Red Hair
-25-

Another Empty Seat, Part 1
-28-

The New Dog Sleeps Like
The Old Dog
-30-

Movie Night #1
-33-

The Ocean and the Beach
-36-

Poem For Jacques (R.I.P.)
-40-

Funeral For Your First Life
-41-

A Few Words For K3
-43-

21 Months
-45-

3 Years Later . . . Lost Friend
-46-

Poem For Domenica (R.I.P.)
-49-

Movie Night #2
-52-

2 Years . . . and Counting
-54-

The (Sort Of) Recurring Dream
-56-

Movie Night #3
-58-

Ghosting
-60-

Up Your Hill
-62-

6 Years Later . . . Lost Friend
-63-

Psychu
-65-

FOMO
-66-

Another Empty Seat, Part 2
-67-

Verify This
-69-

The Southern Wood
-72-

#140
-75-

Middlessence
-76-

Poem 33
-79-

Grave

**A cross
On a clump of dirt
Mourns**

Considerate Crime

We in the West believe in milk.
Snow white, beautifully flavourful,
Filthy rich with calcium,
Super-duper for our teeth, bones
  and hair.

Yes, call us the believers,
Occidental believers in milk.

So much so that we send
A powdered version to Africa:
So that instead of suffering from
  malnutrition,
They can suffer from diarrhea.

Thin Line Between Eating The Crumbs Under The Toaster And Eating What The Cat Dragged In

I can survive, but being careful is so essential. Crying while watching Robin Leach is not foreign in my dwelling, along with bitching at my thousand year-old car (the dinosaur of the speedway), and screaming Carlinisms at my black and blue radio. Times I find myself talking to the mites on the mattress, telling them about my boss and the golf ball clock he has on his office wall. I've given them all names:
Bob walks around freely,
Tina walks around freely,
Janet walks around freely,

In their transistorized world, there are no prisons. Envy courses through my veins: they're invisible beings that exist without human interference. They're born free. I'd love to have their freedom. Give me some!

Give me a break!! Then again, I probably deserve it.

I once thought that being king of the school halls during class was on the same scale with success and happiness. I am presently deciding on whether to have Rice Crispies or Rice Crispies for breakfast.

Maybe they won't repossess my TV, and my co-workers wonder how I got a Visa card. Members of the UMC play killjoy when I get on a high, and college students make me lower my head, and successful old friends make me lie my way in an abyss.

Love In The Eighties

**Love in the Eighties means
Tattooing the word "marriage"
Somewhere on your body
Where you can't see it**

The 24-Year Chasm

What does it take to light the spark? To carry on the vision that one day will be tangible?

In this time of chasm,
   you will find that . . .

Your education gets you so far
Your standards for penetration
   are medium
Your patience is plenty
Your best friend is you
Your best conversations are
   in your head
Your best thoughts and moves
   happen after the fact
Your body rebels and makes you
   sick

Your roads are your escapes
Your travels are all the spice
    you need
Your golf game is average
Your salary will be less that what
    you want it to be
Your "idols" are human and are
    your mirrors
Your regrets are also medium

The end of the abyss is suddenly in
    sight. I know what it takes
    (finally) . . .

A lack of understanding

Your Brittle End

As I eat the pie with 2 friends
   in tow
My thoughts are nowhere near you
As I drink the tea and watch
   the game
My talk is with them not you
You are somewhere invisible to me
Since you don't care to
   communicate
It has been 3 weeks
But you've been silent before
   and returned
Why worry then

On the ice near Dowker Island
The fishermen start their day
They find you there resting
They find you there breathless
The January cold takes that away
As well as your flexibility

No Reasons Why

To know or not know
As your dust sits on a shelf
It will be a No

You Don't Have Red Hair

We meet at a food court
A public place, witnesses
   just in case.
The walking and talking is good
You seem interested
You are attractive, easily had.
You want that food, I want this one
OK, we'll find each other.

(But you don't have red hair)

There you are, sit and talk
Mostly you, it seems like a
   compulsion
Where do my words and opinions
   fit in?
A pregnant friend you recognize
Go say hi, no problem
This could be going better,
   it's still first time.

(But you don't have red hair)

You return, we continue
 conversing
Again, mainly you, but you
 start to relent
Maybe you think I should be equal?
Maybe you have reached
 "the point"
Maybe you have already decided.
I am still interested,
But your "need" for dominance
 worries.

(And you don't have red hair)

Take care, we'll see each other
 again
Absolutely, when I get back
 from Portland
I watch you walk away
Easily had for sure, but that's not
 everything
How weird that makes me at times
But it was there with her,
 not this one.

I don't hear from you anymore
But that's OK
You don't have red hair

Another Empty Seat, Part 1

A man of partial Greek origin
 entertains me
I mostly smile, laughing out loud
 doesn't come.
"I'd call you a cunt, but you neither
 have the depth nor the warmth".
I'll remember that one, and
 probably use it at some point.
He is small but big, voice is meek
 but intelligent
I am satisfied but vacant,
My voice cannot laugh out loud.

Somewhere behind me your
 Mother invisibly sits with a friend,
I don't ask after if she laughed
 out loud,

But I know she enjoyed herself,
   perhaps not fully.
The place seemed full, but not full
   enough,
I sense a theme here.

My left hand touches your
   empty seat
And wishes it was touching
   your thigh.
I know you'd take my hand in yours
And then we'd look at each other
   and smile.
I look to your empty seat and
   get lost in thought,
Until the woman to my right laughs
   out loud.

New Dog Sleeps Like The Old Dog

You are missing something special
  for sure.

The smell of the room rubs badly
  against the joy of the event.
I search for new life, and it's not
  there at first, should be in
  a glass half-bubble with details.
Yet like a dog, he lies on the
  shoulder and chest of
  my Big Man,
Pondering nothing about food or
  bathing or noise (good doggy),
Like he knew it would disturb my
  ideal, initial impression.

Subject matter is surprisingly mixed, not new-life centric at all,
And I selfishly, momentarily hope it stays that way.
But it's more about helpless things now that cry for invisible reasons, and give trouble that you never saw coming.
I desire, perhaps not as much as them, to give permanent love to such dogs that now have homes away from dark wombs.

"I use to sleep with my dog this way".
My thoughts are lost in the past and I'm non-verbal, but the idea for this masterpiece is fertilized.

You missed something special.

Movie Night #1

While waiting for a friend in the lobby of the movie theater last night, two things manifested themselves into more than just fleeting thoughts:

1) Two kids (a boy and girl, about 5-8 years old) are chasing each other around the lobby, playing a combination of tag and hide-and-go-seek, and being generally noisy. Twice they come very close to knocking into me. A parent/guardian is close by and is watching, but is not doing anything to actually control the kids' behaviour.

Is it wrong that the first thought that comes to my mind is to trip one of the kids the next time they come close to me? The other option would be to go over to the parent/guardian and politely ask that they better control the children, but that option is a distance second in my head.

2) Again in the lobby, I start looking closely at a poster for an upcoming movie. I cannot for the life of me remember the name of it, but it looks like a medieval battle type movie. Upon closer reading of the small text, I notice that it says "PG-13: Parental Guidance Strongly Suggested. Contains battle scenes and disturbing images".

Why does this movie get this kind of warning, and yet you can turn on the news any night of the week and see gruesome war footage without any warning? Also, wouldn't you think that after 5 years of the Oil-Grab Iraq War being broadcast on a daily basis, that everyone pretty much has seen enough "battle scenes and disturbing images" to render such movie warnings useless?

The Ocean and the Beach

The Ocean . . . Alone

I am large but feel empty.
The desire to create waves does
   not come easy.
I am mostly clear: you may enter
   and bathe in me,
But I may leave you lonely.
I have been around for some time:
People visit and leave, use me
   for pleasure.
I feel alive yet still, movement will
   cause disturbance and may lead
   to pollution . . . enough of that,
   please.
Your feet may cut themselves on
   some debris: that happens when
   perfection is taken away by the
   times that life leaves in its wake.

My silence yearns for a shore to caress, to bring me to a living place again.

The Beach . . . Alone

As I lie and wait for someone to cool me down,
I try to keep myself clean.
My white sand is still fine to the touch, even after so many years of (mis)use.
Strangers lie on me . . . use me,
Like a bed for their advantage,
Then they leave, possibly to use others like me.
My surface dries under the sun,
The castles slowly erode back into me.
In the distance I see water, dormant for years.

Yet today I feel change:
There is a shiver on my fine skin
As I await what may be.

One

The ocean gently crashes onto the beach.
The water warms and the sand cools.
The dryness moistens and the wetness ensues,
As the water finds its way between the grains.
The crashing continues, interspersed with caressing that fills the emptiness of years past.

And as the steam rises to bring
   joyful pain and then peace,
The injustice of the years
   dissolves away, leaving behind
   lessons learned that will allow for
   a peaceful unity

Poem For Jacques (R.I.P.)

This morning getting ready
   for work
I did not want to shave
I felt I was running behind
One day's stubble was no big deal

As I was having breakfast
I read your obituary
I remembered the occasional
   chats we had across the
   invisible fence

You were the Engineer next door
Asking me how my studies
   were going
Unconsciously encouraging me
   "You can be like me"

I decided to shave

Funeral For Your First Life

Say goodbye to that life
As strange turns change things
And man is quickly slaughtered

More of everything less relaxing
The beaches have gone for now
The occasional trip is less trippy

Certainty is less certain
Cling to things that are
The steps in life are more
  measured
But they get done, as always

Who asks how things are,
When they must see about their
　own lives first?
Or is it poor time management?
Or is it lack of empathy? Both?

You now have a second life
Work at it.

A Few Words For K3

Hello, welcome to our world,
 now yours too.
Less uniformly warm as what
 you've been used to.
Blame our parents, they moved
 here.

Funny how we are wrinkled
 at birth?
Not normally associated with
 youth.

We appreciated the chance to
 come to a hospital for a happy
 occasion for a change.

These other ones around your
   age will grow accustomed to your
   presence.
Share the toys.

I will make fun of you if you ever
   drive a Mercedes Benz.

I hope in time you learn my name
   and my face, and maybe even
   like me.

Until later Oznek . . .

21 Months

Some months are easy
Some are hard
Some are . . . so so

Sometimes I wish I was full of unlimited silver linings
Sometimes my lack of perfection angers me
Sometimes not knowing what to do seems so sad

But one thing I do know . . .

I will continue to be there
Through highs and lows
Mountains and chasms
Heavens and hells

3 Years Later . . . Lost Friend

It hurts less. The rock in my pocket grows smaller, but it is there and probably always will be.

I wonder if you have met my Father and become friends. Both of your minds were affected in different ways. Speak nicely of me.

The Jeopardy Challenge schooled me again, worse than last time. The game we never played screens in my head, although we take turns winning by the thinnest of margins.

The iron ring is still on my finger, found by you amid a myriad of grass blades and darkness.

I wonder how often you thought of me in your final weeks . . . when you exiled me.

The past year was a smattering of minor victories and major hurdles. Please speak to THAT THING to make the days easier for me this year.

I try and treat the girlfriend with as much kindness, respect and love as possible. I wonder if you see any of this and wish it was you.

Your parents miss you, their rocks are bigger I imagine. They visit your island regularly. I have yet to do so, unsure if I want to.
What good would it serve me?

People leave me without saying goodbye. People leave without me saying goodbye. You are part of a growing list . . . enjoy their company while I wonder why.

Ani was better with you. Always something about your first.

HE never would have come back, you could not see that. I've realized that I move on easier, but everyone is not me.

The Indian restaurant is now a Mexican restaurant. I won't go there again.

This day moves on towards Year 4. I promise to continue moving.

Poem For Domenica (R.I.P.)

You were short and stout alive
And you are still that way
Now shinier though unfortunately
You sit quietly while we stare at
   you, perhaps for the last time

All the religion of it hurts me
But Linda and Angi bring reality
I hope you loved and respected
   them

The garden will not be the same
I admired your tenacity with that
But I could have thought of better
   ways to spend my time

I went to bed too early the night
   your daughter was attacked
Her words echoed in my head
   during the service
"I've given you everything!"
I would have helped if I had stayed
   awake

Your intolerance near the end was
   not appreciated
Words travel fast and stay where
   they land
My brain is fertile with opinions
   I do not want
I may forgive you someday,
   whenever that is

I told Bob to let me know if he needed help
I know he won't ask, but it is the kind of thing people always say at those times
I meant it though

If you are somewhere else now
I hope someone always brings you water from a well.

Movie Night #2

A few weeks back, a female friend and I went to the movies. When purchasing tickets, we were told that on this particular night, my ticket would be the regular $11.50, while the friend's ticket would only be $8.00. Reason: it was a "Lady's Night" promotion.

Given my overly egalitarian mindset, the thoughts that passed through my mind (and some that exited my mouth) were:

1) Well that's sexist.

2) Will there be a "Guy's Night" at some point, to keep things fair and equal?

3) Not how I would promote equal rights.

4) You gonna buy me some popcorn with that $3.50 you saved?

2 Years . . . and Counting

And counting . . .
Nice words

All these days
And weeks
And months
And now years,
We are together

I wonder how I succeeded at this,
To keep you happy all this time,
To keep you.
How to continue this positive trend?
How to be supportive at all times?

How do others succeed?
Does anyone ever fully succeed?
Or do we just make our best effort
And hope for the best?

I wonder . . .

The (Sort Of) Recurring Dream

This past week, the dream returned. It is never exactly the same, but the main theme always is. This is about the 5th time this type of dream has happened.

I feel I am in a situation where I have to return to school to finish a course or exam that I did not complete. And of course, I wake up to realize that I have long completed school and I am part of the working world.

Once I felt like I was in high school and I was missing an English class. I even keenly remember one of my English teachers being in the dream. Another time was in university, but I had not written a final exam for a course. It felt like at least a decade had past and I worried how I was going to pass the exam, since after so long I could not remember anything from the course.

The psychologist in me (we all have one) thinks that perhaps I am missing something from my past. Since that feels like too long a list, I think I'll just be content with my life as it is now.

Movie Night #3

So the female friend and I are at the movie theater again (see Movie Night #2). I jokingly wonder aloud if they will have another $8.00 promotion for the ladies, or if this time it will be something for the guys.

Sure enough, same scenario: 1 ticket at regular price of $11.50 and the other reduced to $8.00. The reason this time though: it is a hockey night (Canadiens vs. Maple Leafs), so one of the tickets is reduced in price. Surprisingly though, the woman behind the glass mentions that the reduction is for the woman's ticket.

Excuse me? Are we destroying a stereotype here? I have always thought that it was men who were more into watching sports on TV than women. Therefore, shouldn't the reduction in ticket price be more to entice the guys to go to the movies instead of stay home in front of the television?

Ghosting

You were a victim of ghosting,
  I learned today

As you walk around your small
  apartment
Now so big without me there.
Worrying about your future
Can it work alone? Can it work?

We may always be alone

Your brother reaches out to me
  (you're doing) and I do not grasp
Could I work where he does?
You always painted him as black
Locking you up in the black

Was that true? Am I black too?

You e-mail me while I am on
  a work trip
I ignore, combination of surprise
  and priorities
I eventually answer and we
  occasionally "chat"

Is it still ghosting?

You mainly ignore my reasons
Who are you?
Who were you?
You wonder
My reasons were/are sound
But I caused unnecessary harm

Did you go to the hospital?

It's hard to reach out
It requires confidence and . . .
  confidence

Who's the ghost?

Up Your Hill

I climb towards you with help
You don't know this
The night blinds all
Good, it would seem scary if
  you knew
But I am close and I must know
Eventually I want to come regularly
How can this happen?

I know
You can lust me like I lust you
Feel the connection like I do
Can you try please?

I go down from you
Instead of on you
Temporary depression
Never permanent I think
Will I return?

6 Years Later . . . Lost Friend

I wash the dishes in my kitchen
You are here with your Mom
You talk about something
She is reclining in some fashion
You are upright
You are there.

Still washing dishes
I turn to find your Mom
Kneeling over your dead body
I hear no words though
And the dishes still seem important
Why would you end it there?

But this pill makes the dreams come strong.
I don't want it but my body now heals.
Why can't you just massage me instead?

How is my Father? I care more now than last time. I am still as angry as last time.

The iron ring is tighter on my finger. I blame food and television.

There is no more girlfriend. Did you see that? The quickness with which it all changed?

I saw your parents the night before. You did not come up. But it was not the day. That is today.

It is an Indian restaurant again. I know better ones.

Year 7 . . . lucky me.

Psychu

**It is about you
No, cannot always be you
But still, you are Trump**

FOMO

As the time passes
And the opportunities pass
The sperm gets older
Thankfully you don't feel it

Three begat eight
Four begat nine?
What are the chances?
Slimmer as the years pass

Her name would have been Grace

Another Empty Seat, Part 2

It's a coincidence
The atheist in me screams

We would have gone together
My treat, and I would hope your
    mind would open
Build the bridge and not the wall

But you are not there to know that
    I thought this
Not there in the flesh
When I bought the single ticket
First row balcony, just like you and
    Mom used to do

As the curtain rises and all seats
    are sold
My guest is another empty seat
    to my left
They'll show up, just running late

Act 1 ends, and your emptiness is now here
You came with me it seems, not a coincidence
How does the world do this?
Or why do I think this?

Act 2 ends, and I wish you were here
To anger me with your closed mind
And your silent happiness that I thought of you

Outside the wall,
And I say my goodbyes and return home,
As your echoes push me towards sleep

Verify This

Before you leave
You put 2 condoms in your pocket
Because there was some chemistry
   the first time
And she is probably single

She came into town with work
And you can only hope she comes
   for you as well
Because that is your only chance
   for now
Hopefully after you two have
   dinner

The day went by slowly
You started to think that it will
　not happen
Because that is the trough you are
　currently in
Mentally speaking

Her texts are telling you what you
　predicted
She feels cold and her head hurts
She hopes to be better in time
　for dinner
You wish her well as you feel limp

Outside her hotel in your car
You dial her number in fear
She answers and truly sounds
　down and out
If this is acting it is very good

No problem next time you say
Will there be a next time
There is always a next time
   in your mind
Where the world is your stage

The food dulls the pain
For a brief moment you eat your
   emotions
And as you pay your bill
You realize you are the only one
   there alone

The Southern Wood

Part 1

You had recently parted ways
   with your man
I was there as a "friend" who filled
   the empty spaces
There was chemistry that no
   chemist could create
Remember the deck?
How I was there for support?
Funny how I don't remember
   how it ended
Actually, it's not funny.

Part 2

You call, and I come . . . over
It rained hard the night you
   wanted us again
With the windows and your
   lips open
We reclaimed our mutual wanting
And again, it eventually ended,
   your doing
But I remember this one and why,
   I understood
As we held each other the last time
Which I hoped was not the
   last time

Part 3

Some of me always wants to fly
   and see you
To that city you now live close to
(The one that rhymes with a
   body part)
Work, life, death, family,
   children, exes . . . oh yes,
   and indecision, all get in the way

#140

Is that all you can give?
Using big words too hard?
Being compassionate too hard?
Not being a racist too hard?
What say you POTUS?
Little

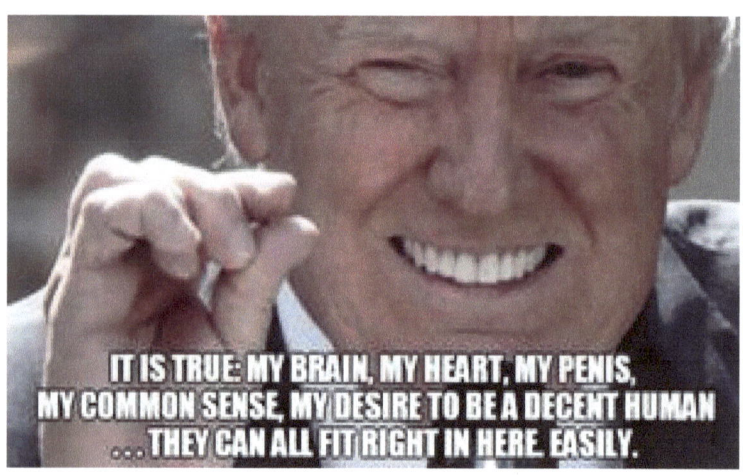

Middlessence

Making it up from bed
It seems harder as time goes by
Denseness in the back
Dragging the physical and
   mental being
Little by little chipping away
Easy how you see the
   negative nowadays
Although never quitting the routine
Good for you my darling boy
Egg yourself on and go work
   for whatever

See yourself for what you are
Edging closer to death
   and farther from youth
Leave some room for joy
Festering beneath layers of Ifs
Does that make you a realist?
Or just a run of the mill pessimist?
Unsure of the way things will go
But it has always worked
   out somehow
Try to be positive for you and all

Return to the place that makes sense
Engage in things that bring that fleeting joy
Adapt to the oncoming unknown
Divert your eyes from the attention whores
Justify the choices and bring some luck to the table
Use them with respect and they will still like you
Surrender to the groove of a life still breathing
Threaten the status quo with painless violence
Meet them halfway when absolutely necessary
Entertain the fact that it is never over
Nestle into the world of now and begin motion
Time to live

Poem 33

**And with you it ends
I was stubborn about it
But you still matter**

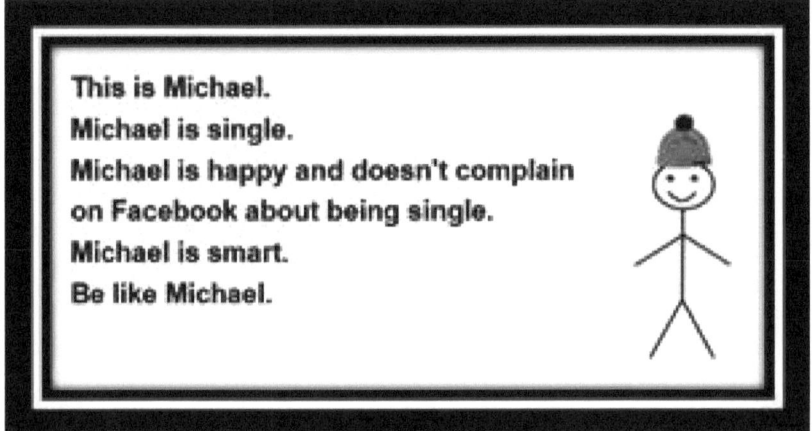

Note by the Poet

Fellow Readers,

Thank you very much for showing interest in my book. It is my first one, and I hope not the last. We'll see what life brings won't we!

When I first started writing many years ago, it was a way for me to express myself in a way that I often could not do by voice: I found it easier to get my point across with my words on paper than from my tongue. Even today, I still find it to be my stronger method of communication, although the need to live a sociable life has rendered my oral communication skills much stronger.

In recent years, when I picked up the pen again (actually, it was more like turning on the computer!), I found that the feelings/thoughts/opinions I had gathered over the years had to land somewhere. As well, the feeling that a published book was something within my capabilities yet never achieved, drove me towards realizing this goal that could honestly have happened much earlier.

Well, better late than never at all.

So once again, thank you showing interest in my written voice.

All the best and none of the worst to you.

www.ingramcontent.com/pod-product-compliance
Lightning Source LLC
Chambersburg PA
CBHW042305150426
43197CB00001B/24